New SAT Strategies for a 1600

By
Nathan Halberstadt

Author: Nathan Halberstadt
Editor: Damian Castaneda
Cover by Nathan Halberstadt

Printed in the United States of America
First Printing, 2017
ISBN: 978-1549527135

amazon.com/author/nathanhalberstadt

CONTENTS

Introduction: The Goal

Step 1: Aim High

Success on the SAT doesn't happen because of luck. It's predictable *if* you follow a plan. This book is your plan.

Let's aim high by creating a specific goal to shoot for. Here's what you need to do:

1. Get out a sheet of paper and a pencil

2. Make a list of schools you want to get accepted into.

3. Write down the average SAT score of each college next to its name.

4. Circle the school you most want to attend.

5. The average SAT score from your favorite school is your goal.

You will need to work hard to achieve the average SAT score from your favorite school.

Step 2: Practice from *Real* Tests—Your #1 Strategy

The secret to SAT success is taking *real* practice tests. A *real* test is an actual SAT exam from a previous year released by the College Board. It's not some artificial grouping of questions from a book or private company. And it's not tests from the old SAT because those questions are different from the New SAT and are irrelevant.

Practice tests may seem boring, and you may be looking for some other secret formula. But mastering the *real* practice tests is the most important secret to SAT success. Do I need to repeat that? **It's your #1 strategy to success**. Why? Because the New SAT uses the same questions over and over again. It's a pattern. It has to be a pattern because the exam is scaled based on past exams. The examiners want your SAT experience to be very similar to students who took it in the past. You will likely run into many nearly identical questions every time you take the SAT. The real practice exams are the most similar to what you will see on the day of the SAT. So duh. Practice from real questions. I'll explain exactly how to do this in more detail later on in the book.

Studying vs. Practicing. Studying is not the same as practicing. Studying is passive learning. Doing questions and reviewing the right and wrong answers is active learning. Here's the key: knowing why the wrong answers are wrong is just as important if not more important than knowing why the right answers are right.

So don't fall prey to the lie that you need to read a gazillion pages of material before you are ready to start taking practice SAT exams. That's the biggest mistake you can make. Remember, studying is passive learning. It's not the real thing unless you are practicing with real SAT test questions.

Reality Check. Don't expect to do too well on practice tests. The SAT repeats the same questions, so you will eventually get the right answers as you continue to practice.

If you start getting upset with your progress, remember this: you're not supposed to do well on practice tests. Instead, expect that you will fail to achieve your score on your practice exams. That's why it's called a *practice* exam. You are not supposed to know the answers. You're only supposed to understand why you missed answers. So make sure you study both the right and wrong answers. Understanding why the wrong answers are wrong is just as important as understanding why the right answers are right.

If you can't find any motivation to study, just take out your sheet of paper. Look at your goal. Remember, if you put in the work, you can achieve it.

Make A Reasonable Goal

The first time I took the SAT I received a score of 1320. I was unhappy with my score. So I decided to learn how to master the test from the inside out. As the time came for me to take the SAT, I diligently prepared for four weeks. My goal was to score a 1550 because I wanted to be accepted into a top 20 university such as Stanford University where my older brother attended for his undergraduate degree in mechanical engineering.

When I took the SAT again after having prepared for four weeks, I scored a 1560—10 points higher than my goal. This score put me in the 99th percentile and absolutely changed my outlook as far as which colleges I could be accepted into. Right now I am only 17 years old. I am approaching the time when I will start applying for colleges, and I am only beginning to comprehend the significance the improvement in my SAT score will have on my life as it opens up new doors for me.

What follows is a concise book revealing several simple tactics that will improve your score that I discovered while preparing for the SAT.

Two Schedules To Choose From

At the end of the book there are two schedules from which you need to choose one depending on how much time you have until the test date. Follow the plan exactly in your preparation for the SAT. The plan is identical to what I did when I prepared for the SAT. I believe that I am uniquely qualified to teach how to do well on this exam because I just took the exam this year. Other SAT tutors have not taken the SAT in perhaps a dozen years, and back then the SAT was far different than it is now. As someone who has just gone through the SAT process I believe that I can provide fresh insight to help any student improve their score by at least 150 points or get into the 99th percentile if they follow my method.

Chapter 1

The Format of the Test

In order to understand the strategies and advice in the rest of this book, you must first know the format of the test. This test is broken up into five portions each with a set time limit. You can only work on each specified portion of the test during its allotted time. I will go into more detail on each section of the test later in this book, but for now I will give you a brief overview.

- Reading: 65 minutes
  - 5-10 minute break
- Writing: 35 minutes
- Math Non-Calculator: 25 minutes
  - 5-10 minute break
- Math Calculator: 55 minutes

- o 2 minute break

- Essay: 50 minutes

The reading and writing sections of the test combine to form a reading/writing score out of 800. The math non-calculator and math calculator sections of the test combine to form a math score of 800. The essay is scored on its own out of 24.

On the reading section of the test, you will read five passages and answer a total of fifty-two questions. These questions will focus on critical reading. The questions will ask about the author's point, what certain clauses mean, and what certain words mean.

In the writing section of the test, you will read four passages and answer a total of forty-two questions. These questions are focused on grammar, specifically correcting mistakes in the passages.

In the math non-calculator section of the test, you will answer a total of twenty questions. The first fifteen of these questions will be multiple choice, and the last five will be open response. The questions start off easy and get progressively harder. Be sure to be past halfway through the questions when half of the time is passed because the later questions are harder and require more time. Once you get to the last five questions, the open response questions, the difficulty resets and the questions become easy, but they quickly get harder again as you approach the end of the section.

In the math calculator section of the test, you will answer a total of thirty-eight questions. The first thirty of these questions will be multiple choice, and the last eight will be open response. The questions once again start off easy and get progressively harder. Be sure to be past halfway through the questions when half of the time is passed because the later questions are harder and require more time. Once you get to the last eight questions, the open response questions, the difficulty resets and the questions become easy, but they quickly get harder again as you approach the end of the section.

In the essay, you read a passage and prepare and write a rhetorical strategies essay in fifty minutes. Later on in the book I will explain how exactly to write a rhetorical strategies essay if you are unsure.

Chapter 2

Marking up the Book

The most basic SAT strategy is marking up the your test booklet. You must put the pencil to the paper at every possible opportunity. Your memory is not as great as you think it is. If you do not write while you test, you will quickly forget things you wanted to remember and be forced to reread material. Every time you read an answer choice, either cross it out, or put a small dot next to it. Cross an answer choice out if you know it is wrong. Put a small dot next to an answer choice if you think it could be right. Once you have gone through all four answer choices, you should have crossed out three and dotted one. If this is the case, circle the dotted one in the test booklet and move on to the next question. Too many students waste time rereading the answer choices, questions, and texts over and over. You never want to have to read something twice. The above method will work for almost every question.

In a case where you end up with two dotted answer choices and two crossed out answer choices, focus on the two dotted answer choices and decide between those. If you end up crossing out all of the answer choices, reread the question and all of the choices to figure out what you do not understand. It is important that you circle your answer choice in the test booklet as it relates to strategy 2.

In the math sections you absolutely must write out your work. If you try to do problems in your head, you will make silly errors which when added up will massively damage your score.

In the reading and writing sections you must underline and annotate the passages as you read. Although underlining and annotating may seem like a waste of time, marking the text will help your brain to focus and actually comprehend what you are reading. Have you ever read a page in a book and realized that you did not remember a single thing on the page? Underlining will prevent this from happening on the test.

When I was preparing to take the SAT, my test booklet would be littered with marks. If you are struggling to do well on the SAT, try writing all over the book. I guarantee that you will see immediate improvement in your testing.

?

Chapter 3

Bubble Trouble—the Right Way to Bubble

This simple trick is a personal favorite of mine, and it will save you loads of time on the test. *Only fill in the bubbles on the answer sheet after you have completed a full page in the test booklet.* Do not fill in a bubble after every question. Answer all of the questions on a given page by circling the right answer in the test booklet as you work your way through the questions one after the next without breaking focus even for a second. Once you have finished the page, relax your focus for about twenty seconds while you copy your circled answers onto the bubble sheet. You can think of the short bubbling break as a well-earned reward for your hard work on the page you just finished.

Breaking up the test like this makes the mental strain much more manageable while simultaneously saving you time because you remain more focused. If you go back and forth between test booklet and answer sheet between every question, the switching back and forth will make it difficult for you to focus and slow you down considerably on the test. I predict that this strategy alone of bubbling only once you have finished a page will save you at least 5 minutes of time on each of the four multiple choice sections on the test because of improved focus. Be sure to try this tactic on your next practice test and see if you finish with improved scores and with more time remaining than usual.

Chapter 4

Making a Good Guess

Always guess on problems that you are struggling with and then move on quickly. There is no point penalty for guessing wrong on the new SAT, so you must always guess. You should not spend more than one minute on any given problem. Since you are marking up the answer choices, if you are struggling with a problem you hopefully will have eliminated (by crossing out) at least one or two answer choices. Simply pick one of the remaining dotted answer choices and move on as quickly as possible. Put a star next to this question that you were unsure about so that you can come back to it if you finish the section with time left. Remember that ideally you will have time to come back to it at the end of the section.

It is important to note that when you come back to a problem after having completed a section, you will likely realize the correct answer quickly because now you are reading the question afresh. This is a far better system than spending five minutes getting nowhere on a single problem. Your time could be better used elsewhere. Never spend more than a minute on a problem. Always keep moving. Do not waste too much of your time on hard problems that you might never get correct because that time could be spent answering all of the easy questions.

If you are working on a section and realize with one minute left that you will not be able to finish, you must stop working and bubble in the rest of the answers on the section at random. I would recommend bubbling the same letter for all of them to save time. If you have 4 questions left, just bubble "A" for all four and then maybe in the last 30 seconds you can figure out what one of the answers is for those four.

Use every second up to when the time ends. If you finish a section with time left, go back and check as many problems as you can. You should never be just sitting there waiting for your time to be up. This test is very important, and you need to put every ounce of your effort into this for the three hours that you will be testing.

Chapter 5

Practicing with College Board Tests

Practice makes perfect. Take all eight of the official College Board released practice tests before your test date. These strategies will only help you if you practice regularly. If you are someone who is taking the SAT one or two months from now, I recommend that you take one of the five sections of the SAT every day using the exact amount of time that you are officially allowed for the given section. I would also recommend that you wake up early on a Saturday and take a *full* released SAT from start to finish with the exact time restraints of the real test. You should do this at least twice before exam day, preferably one of them the Saturday a week before exam day so that you are accustomed to testing for several hours early in the morning.

I would recommend that you buy the latest edition of the College Board book full of practice tests. Alternatively, you could print out all eight of the released SAT tests (double sided), and print out eight copies of the answer sheets. This does consume loads of paper and ink, so I would recommend going to a store to print, although you could just do it at home. If you don't have the College Board book, you must print out the SAT test booklets and answer sheets. You do not need to print out the answer keys.

Practicing from the computer screen will not help your SAT score in any dramatic way. You must practice exactly the same way that you will test. It is important that you use the College Board released exams. These exams are the most similar to what you will see on the day of the SAT. In fact, you will likely run into some nearly identical questions on the real SAT.

As you probably know, there are practice tests made by other companies (such as Princeton Review and Barron's) and these can be helpful. But these tests made by other companies should only be used if you have exhausted the supply of official College Board released tests. Remember that the official College Board released tests are made by the same people who will be writing your exam. You can find the released tests on the College Board website. The link below will take you there or just Google "college board new sat practice tests", and it will be the first result.

https://collegereadiness.collegeboard.org/sat/practice/full-length-practice-tests

Chapter 6

Never Making the Same Mistake Twice

Go over wrong answers repeatedly. Make sure that you will never again miss an answer that you previously got wrong. Once you have finished a section of a released College Board exam, grade the section from the online answer key, and spend time figuring out how to do the problems you missed. Correcting and analyzing missed problems is how you will improve for the next time you take the full test.

One convenient aspect of the SAT is that questions tend to be extraordinarily similar from test to test. If you can master every question type, there will be no surprises on the exam and you will know the fastest way to solve every problem the moment you see it on exam day. Thus, it is imperative that you learn from your mistakes and that you don't get the same answers wrong over and over again. You need to shoot for perfection.

Fifteen minutes should be spent every day reviewing wrong answers. The College Board provides answer explanations for every question on all eight of the released online tests if you are unsure of what you did wrong. If the answer explanations online are not enough, don't be afraid to ask a sibling, parent, friend, or teacher for help on any given problem.

Chapter 7

Reading Strategies

For many people, the reading section is the most difficult part of the test. If you struggle with finishing this section in the set amount of time, there are several tips and tricks that can make this section more manageable.

Answer questions as you read. Most people read a whole passage through and then answer the questions afterwards. When they answer the questions, they have to reread the passage about five more times as they search for the answers to each individual question. Fortunately, there is a better method. Do not read the passage and then answer the questions as most people do. Instead, *answer the questions that have line references first as you read through the* *passage*. Answer main idea questions last. To clarify, do *not* start to read the passage until you have read the first question with a line reference. Proceed to work your way through the passage for the first time as you answer questions. Now, this may seem confusing at first and probably like a bad idea to you. But if done correctly, this is the best way to ensure that you get all the answers correct in the shortest amount of time possible.

Many of the questions have line references and these questions are always in order from beginning to end. For example, if there are ten questions on a given passage, the first question might ask about line 9, the third question about line 21, the fourth question about line 42, and the seventh question about line 60. As you can see, the questions work their way through the passage. This allows you to work through the passage while you are answering questions. Simply look for the first question with a line reference (for example, line 9) and then read up through line 9. Now answer the first question. Then continue reading up through the line reference (for example line 21) of the question three and continue doing this until you have answered all the questions with line references.

Once you have finished answering all of the questions with line references, you will have finished reading the passage. Now, go back and answer the big picture questions. These should be easy to answer since you have just read the whole passage and already dissected the detailed questions. At this point, copy all of your circled answers from the test booklet onto the answer sheet.

Question Pairs of 2. Often times there will be a question asking for the main purpose of the passage followed by another question saying "what line best supports your answer to the last question?" When you are answering these question pairs, use the line references in the second question to answer the first question. One of the line references in the second question will contain the answer to the first question.

Be interested in the passages. If you have to, pretend you are interested. You do this all the time with your friends, so don't be shy about doing it now. Sometimes the passages may seem boring. Strike that. The passages are *always* boring. This is intentional because the examiners want you to get bored and lose focus. You probably don't care about the migrational patterns of the African Swallow. But for the few minutes that you are spending reading the passage, you must convince yourself that you really do care. Pretend that you are an expert in the field and that every detail profoundly affects your life. Or when you just read the most boring sentence ever, think to yourself, "How cool" or "How interesting". "Whatever" should not pop into your head as you read. But it should pop into your head after the test.

Most Answer Choices Are Wrong. If you can find any reason why you think one answer might be wrong, it's definitely wrong. The right answer is always unquestionably right—like your parents. Sometimes the SAT writers will try to trick you by creating answers that seem right except for just one little detail in the passage that would contradict the answer. If you see a detail that makes an answer choice wrong, cross out the answer choice! It's wrong!

Chapter 8

Writing Strategies read all

Déjà vu. In the writing section, you should also answer questions as your read just like you did with the reading section. There simply isn't enough time to read the whole passage and then go back to answer questions.

Grammar Review. A decent level of grammatical knowledge is essential for this section of the test. In this chapter, I will gloss over a lot of grammatical material that you should know. This is meant to be a refresher of material that you already know. If this material is new to you, you have some studying to do.

First, you must know the difference between the following pairs of similar words. The SAT writers will often try to trick you by using the wrong one of many of the following pairs:

affect	Verb "studying <u>affects</u> your scores"
effect	Noun "the <u>effects</u> of studying are good"
than	Comparison "he is better <u>than</u> me at this"
then	Conjunction "<u>then</u> I went to the store"
Its, your, their, whose	Possessive "put away <u>your</u> phone"
It's, you're, they're, who's	It is, you are, they are, who is "<u>you're</u> fun to hang out with"
I	I does the action "<u>I</u> bought those shoes"
me	Me receives the action "he gave it to <u>me</u>"
imminent	Coming "he is in <u>imminent</u> danger"
eminent	Famous "the <u>eminent</u> singer"
compliment	Tell a person something nice "she <u>complimented</u> me"
complement	To go well together "those shoes <u>complement</u> your dress"

The most clear and concise answer is always right. Often times in the writing section, the authors will ask you how to fix a sentence or how to combine two sentences. The answer choice that is the least wordy will be correct without fail. Often times the one in the active voice is correct. Stay out of the passive voice if it can be helped. If a sentence feels too wordy, it's probably wrong.

Be careful of constructions where the same idea is repeated. For example, if a sentence says "he looked intelligent and smart." You need to delete the "and smart" or the "intelligent and" in order to make the sentence correct.

You need to know the following rules for punctuation marks:

Semicolons:

Rule 1: Use semicolons to join two independent clauses. Use them to replace the combination of a comma and coordinating conjunction. The coordinating conjunctions are *and, but, for, or, nor, so, and yet.*

Example: I walked my dog this morning; it was cold.

Notice how the semicolon could be replaced by a comma and coordinating conjunction. *I walked my dog this morning, and it was cold.* You can always replace a semicolon with a comma and a coordinating conjunction

Rule 2: Use semicolons instead of commas in a list that already contains commas.

Example: *You should eat dinner with a fork, which is for the main course; with a knife, which is for cutting; and a spoon, which is for the soup.*

Note: Be careful not to confuse semicolons with colons. The SAT writers always include questions where they use a semicolon instead of a colon and vice-versa to see if you will catch it.

Colons:

Rule 1: Introduce an item with a colon.

Example: *I want one item from the store: milk.*

Rule 2: Introduce a list with a colon.

Example: *I want the following items from the store: milk, eggs, butter, and sugar.*

Dashes:

Rule 1: Introduce an item with a dash.

Example: *I want one item from the store—milk.*

Rule 2: Introduce a list with a dash

Example: *I want the following items from the store—milk, eggs, butter, and sugar.*

Rule 3: Use a dash before and after a phrase of nonessential information instead of parentheses or commas.

Example: *When I met the members of the band—all four of them—I took a selfie with them.*

Note: As you can see, colons and dashes function almost identically, but semicolons and colons are entirely different. You should never confuse semicolons and colons.

Comma rules:

Rule 1: Use a comma to connect two independent clauses with a comma and a coordinating conjunction. The coordinating conjunctions are *and, but, for, or, nor, so, and yet.*

Example: *I went to the store, and I saw my friend there.*

Rule 2: Use a comma after an introductory prepositional phrase

Example: *After my run this morning, I ate a banana.*

Rule 3: Use a comma after an introductory dependent clause. Dependent means that it cannot stand on its own. Just like you can't live on your own yet without your parents help. You are dependent on your parents. And the Cleveland Cavaliers are dependent on Lebron James.

Look at this sentence: "If you want to come with me" is not a complete sentence. Why not? Think about it. If your friend said that to you, you would say, "If I want to come with you where? Speak in complete sentences dude." It's a dependent clause because the clause needs more information for you to know what the person is talking about. So it needs a comma after it. If the dependent clause comes first before the independent clause, you need a comma after the dependent clause. On the other hand, if the sentence order is reversed and the dependent clause comes after the independent clause, you do *not* use a comma.

Example 1: *If you want to come with me, you should change out of your pajamas or pay me $50.*

In example 1, you have the dependent clause before the independent clause, so you need a comma.

Example 2: *You should change out of your pajamas if you want to come with me.*

In example 2, you have the dependent clause after the independent clause, so no comma.

Rule 4: Use commas to separate 3 or more items in a list.

Example: *Mom told me to clean the cupboard, desk, table, and carpet.*

Rule 5: Use commas before and after nonessential information that could otherwise be put in parenthesis or deleted without changing the meaning of the sentence.

Example: *My friend, who is 2 years older than me, wants to be a surgeon.*

Rule 6: Use commas to separate two or more adjectives describing the same noun.

Example: *The clear, blue sky is beautiful.*

Rule 7: Use a comma after a subordinate conjunction. There are many subordinate conjunctions including the following: accordingly, again, also, besides, consequently, finally, for example, further, furthermore, hence, however, indeed, in fact, instead, likewise, moreover, namely, nevertheless, otherwise, still, that is, then, therefore, and thus.

Example: *However, I do want to study tonight.*

Rule 8: Use commas for other miscellaneous reasons such as for dates or geographical names.

Example: *We plan on going to Rochester, New York on November 6, 2018.*

There are more comma rules, but these are the most important ones to know. The SAT writers tend to put in unnecessary commas, so be ready to delete extra commas on the SAT.

Chapter 9

Math Strategies

Good news folks. The SAT math section is easy and predictable. It's just algebra with a little bit of geometry sprinkled in. Don't overuse your calculator on the Math calculator section. This stuff isn't rocket science. Your calculator is not needed for 75% of the problems. The test writers want to test if you know when it's appropriate to use a calculator. Make sure that you are still writing the problems out on paper in the calculator section of the SAT.

Plug in. If you don't know how to quickly solve a problem, plug in numbers from the answer choices into the given equation. This little tip often helps if you are stuck. Basically, do the problem backwards. Remember that the answer is in front of you.

Always Write an Equation. Most of the math section consists of word problems. You need to make equations out of all of these word problems. Turn the words into symbols and numbers. Then solving is just basic algebra.

Math Terms. You must know how to calculate the mean, median, mode, range, and standard deviation of a set of numbers.

Mean	Average. "The average person is mean."
Median	Arrange all numbers in order from the smallest to greatest and pick the middle number. "The freeway median is in the middle."
Mode	The number that occurs the most often in a list or set of data.
Range	The biggest number minus the smallest number.
Standard Deviation	How far away from the average the numbers are in a set. A small standard deviation means that the numbers are close to the average. A large standard deviation means that the numbers are far from the average.

There are of course a great number of details and concepts that are important to know for the math section, and these can be ironed out only through practice. It is exceedingly important in the math sections to understand why you get questions wrong and to never repeat the same mistakes. There are only a few dozen concepts that they test, so as you practice you will eventually memorize how to answer every question type. At that point, you will be more than prepared to achieve an 800 on the SAT Math section.

If you want to solidify your math skills, prepare for the SAT II Math 2 subject test as you are practicing for the SAT. Taking this subject test for college admissions is a great idea, and more importantly, taking this test and preparing for this test will make the SAT math sections feel like a walk in the park. If you can get to the point where you can score in the 700s on the SAT II Math 2 subject test, you are easily within striking distance of getting an 800 on the Math section of the SAT. If you have not taken the prerequisite math courses for the Math 2 subject test, you should at least consider taking the SAT II Math 1 subject test.

Chapter 10

Essay Strategies

Importance: The essay is the least important section because it's not factored into your 1600 score. Some colleges don't even ask for the essay; however, many colleges will take notice if your essay score is unusually low or high. And since you are shooting for the highest possible score of 24, the colleges you want to get into *will* care. So you should care too.

Don't concern yourself with the low standard some colleges set. You are reading this because you don't want to be average. If you have the talent and desire to be your best, go for the maximum score of 24. Be your best in everything you do. Writing skills are perhaps the most important skills you can acquire.

Format: The essay is graded out of 24 possible points by two graders who each give you a score from 1 to 12 and then add up the two scores. There are three categories on the essay, each with a possible 4 points from each grader: reading, analysis and writing. In order to get a perfect score on the essay, you just need to maximize your performance in these three criteria. All you have to do is check the rubric boxes. You do not have to write the best essay ever in order to do well on the essay section. Most importantly, relax. The essay is the easiest section on the SAT.

The SAT essay is a rhetorical strategies essay. This means that you will read an essay or speech and analyze the argument that is being made in the speech. Many students go into the SAT test room not even knowing how to properly write a rhetorical strategies essay. A little explanation and some examples will clear up any fear or confusion that you may have.

Your Approach: Your first step when you approach the essay is to skip the directions. Remember that you only have fifty minutes to prepare and write your essay so every minute saved counts in your favor. The directions are long and always the same. Read them once through now and then never read them again:

The essay gives you an opportunity to show how effectively you can read and comprehend a passage and write an essay analyzing the passage. In your essay, you should demonstrate that you have read the passage carefully, present a clear and logical analysis, and use language precisely.

Your essay must be written on the lines provided in your answer booklet; except for the planning page of the answer booklet, you will receive no other paper on which to write. You will have enough space if you write on every line, avoid wide margins, and keep your handwriting to a reasonable size. Remember that people who are not familiar with your handwriting will read what you write. Try to write or print so that what you are writing is legible to those readers.

You have 50 minutes to read the passage and write an essay in response to the prompt provided inside this booklet.

1. *Do not write your essay in this booklet. Only what you write on the lined pages of your answer booklet will be evaluated.*

2. *An off-topic essay will not be evaluated.*

As you read the passage below, consider how [the author] uses evidence, such as facts or examples, to support claims, reasoning to develop ideas and to connect claims and evidence, stylistic or persuasive elements, such as word choice or appeals to emotion, to add power to the ideas expressed.

[passage]

Write an essay in which you explain how [the author] builds an argument to persuade his/her audience of [the author's purpose]. In your essay, analyze how [the author] uses one or more of the features listed in the box above (or features of your own choice) to strengthen the logic and persuasiveness of his argument. Be sure that your analysis focuses on the most relevant features of the passage.

Your essay should not explain whether you agree with [the author's] claims, but rather explain how [the author] builds an argument to persuade his/her audience.

Now that you have read the directions, you can discard them from your brain. The directions don't do a great job of explaining what you really need to do. On test day just imagine all the other students reading through that mess of directions for five minutes while you instead dive right into your well prepared essay.

When you sit down to write the essay, you need to jump right into reading the passage given. While you are reading you need to underline rhetorical strategies. What are rhetorical strategies? Rhetorical strategies are tactics that make the author's argument more effective. Maybe in your English class you have talked about some rhetorical strategies. Some examples of rhetorical strategies include:

Appeal to authority	Hyperbole	Metaphor
Appeal to emotion	Warning of consequences	Descriptions
Appeal to reason	Word choice	Telling a short story
Appeal to logic	Citing data	Contrasting

You will write a five paragraph essay with each of the three body paragraphs focusing on one rhetorical strategy and how it is used in the piece to make the author's argument stronger. As you read through the passage you will need to underline at least two examples of each of three different rhetorical strategies that you chose. Make yourself an expert at the rhetorical strategies you feel most comfortable with. In my experience, it is easiest to use word choice, citing data, and appeal to emotion on the SAT exam. Of course, you should use whichever strategies work best in the given piece, but often you can use whichever rhetorical strategies you want because the passages that they provide will always be loaded with rhetorical strategies.

An example body paragraph would probably be helpful to you. Here is an example body paragraph that I wrote under a strict time limit when I was preparing for the SAT:

Klinenberg expertly supports his argument by employing clever word choices. Most ironically, he says that Americans should "put [their] air conditioning on ice" (Klinenberg 6) in a thoughtful clincher intended to bring a smile to the reader's face as he drives his point home. He uses this rhetorical strategy to rephrase his thesis that we need to stop using air conditioners in excess to save the planet. In another instance, he says that "the case for air-condition is made of air" (Klinenberg 3). Clearly, Klinenberg feels that no argument for the use of air-conditioning could stand up to scrutiny. The astute use of word choice adds color through irony to the work, which in turn helps to convince the reader that they need to reduce their reliance on air-conditioning.

OK, so the paragraph above is pretty short. And you're probably thinking, "that's not even a good paragraph". Admittedly, the paragraph above is far from perfect, and it *is* quite short. But that's ok! The graders aren't looking for perfection.

It's just an example of the format that you will want to follow. Write a topic sentence where you claim that the author uses a rhetorical strategy to support his/her argument. Then quote at least two portions of the passage that are examples of the rhetorical strategy, and be sure to cite the quotations with (author last name, line number). After each quotation explain how the quoted section supports the author's argument. Close with the author's thesis. Rinse and repeat twice with different rhetorical strategies of your choice for the next two body paragraphs.

Your introduction and conclusion paragraphs should be similar to each other. Begin with a thesis. Add an optional sentence or two of your choice, and then finish the paragraph with a sentence where you say what rhetorical strategies you will use. The College Board wants concise introductions and conclusions.

If you can properly present the author's main point in your thesis you will likely successfully get all 8 points in the reading criteria. In order to do well on the reading section you need to demonstrate that you understand the passage that you are reading. Fortunately the author's main point is always described in the boxed instruction blurb of text after the passage. Simply rephrase what you read in this boxed text in order to plug into the last portion of your thesis. So your introduction should look something like this:

In [passage title], [author name] sets out to convince his/her audience of his/her conviction that [rephrased author point which you can find in the boxed in instructions after the passage] in response to [opposing view on topic]. [author last name] effectively creates his/her argument by using [list three rhetorical strategies].

Feel free to add one or two more sentences into your introduction and conclusion between the two sentences laid out above. Just remember that it is fine if these paragraphs are short. If you still feel nervous about the essay, I would suggest reading example essays online and doing your best to imitate them in style and form. Below is an example of a perfect scoring essay that College Board provided:

In response to our world's growing reliance on artificial light, writer Paul Bogard argues that natural darkness should be preserved in his article "Let There be dark". He effectively builds his argument by using a personal anecdote, allusions to art and history, and rhetorical questions.

Bogard starts his article off by recounting a personal story – a summer spent on a Minnesota lake where there was "woods so dark that [his] hands disappeared before [his] eyes." In telling this brief anecdote, Bogard challenges the audience to remember a time where they could fully amass themselves in natural darkness void of artificial light. By drawing in his readers with a personal encounter about night darkness, the author means to establish the potential for beauty, glamour, and awe-inspiring mystery that genuine darkness can possess. He builds his argument for the preservation of natural darkness by reminiscing for his readers a first-hand encounter that proves the "irreplaceable value of darkness." This anecdote provides a baseline of sorts for readers to find credence with the author's claims.

Bogard's argument is also furthered by his use of allusion to art – Van Gogh's "Starry Night" – and modern history – Paris' reputation as "The City of Light". By first referencing "Starry Night", a painting generally considered to be undoubtedly beautiful, Bogard establishes that the natural magnificence of stars in a dark sky is definite. A world absent of excess artificial light could potentially hold the key to a grand, glorious night sky like Van Gogh's according to the writer. This urges the readers to weigh the disadvantages of our world consumed by unnatural, vapid lighting. Furthermore, Bogard's alludes to Paris as "the famed 'city of light'". He then goes on to state how Paris has taken steps to exercise more sustainable lighting practices. By doing this, Bogard creates a dichotomy between Paris' traditionally alluded-to name and the reality of what Paris is becoming – no longer "the city of light", but moreso "the city of light...before 2 AM". This furthers his line of argumentation because it shows how steps can be and are being taken to preserve natural darkness. It shows that even a city that is literally famous for being constantly lit can practically *address light pollution in a manner that preserves the beauty of both the city itself and the universe as a whole.*

Finally, Bogard makes subtle yet efficient use of rhetorical questioning to persuade his audience that natural darkness preservation is essential. He asks the readers to consider "what the vision of the night sky might inspire in each of us, in our children or grandchildren?" in a way that brutally plays to each of our emotions. By asking this question, Bogard draws out heartfelt ponderance from his readers about the affecting power of an untainted night sky. This rhetorical question tugs at the readers' heartstrings; while the reader may have seen an unobscured night skyline before, the possibility that their child or grandchild will never get the chance sways them to see as Bogard sees. This strategy is definitively an appeal to pathos, forcing the audience to directly face an emotionally-charged inquiry that will surely spur some kind of response. By doing this, Bogard develops his argument, adding gutthral power to the idea that the issue of maintaining natural darkness is relevant and multifaceted.

Writing as a reaction to his disappointment that artificial light has largely permeated the presence of natural darkness, Paul Bogard argues that we must preserve true, unaffected darkness. He builds this claim by making use of a personal anecdote, allusions, and rhetorical questioning.

Chapter 11

Read Like a Pro

Read often. Read daily. Force yourself to read for at least thirty minutes each day. At first it will be difficult, but once reading is a habit, it becomes fun. It would be best if you could read academic articles, but even reading fiction would be helpful for the SAT. Reading daily will improve your attention span, vocabulary size, reading comprehension, reading speed, writing skills, grammatical accuracy, and in general will make you much more comfortable on the SAT. Think of reading daily as a workout regiment that will get you stronger for the SAT. Even if you are taking the SAT only a few days from now, beginning the habit of reading daily will have immediate benefits on your SAT score. If you are taking the SAT in a few months, reading every day from now until the day before the test will enable you to improve your SAT score.

On the reading section of the SAT, the passages are a mixture of historical documents, excerpts from novels, and scientific journals. You will encounter:

- One excerpt from a modern novel
- One historical document or historical speech
- One modern academic selection on economics or other social studies
- One science passage
- One pair of side by side science passages which you will have to compare and contrast

It's important that in your free reading you diversify what you are reading. If you chose to read a novel, that's great! But be sure to also read some science articles in order to familiarize yourself with the style of academic scientific journals. The historical documents will often employ various forms of older English that may be difficult to understand if you are not accustomed to the style. With this in mind, I would also recommend that you read some books from the 1700s in order to freshen up your comprehension for the SAT. Below is

a list of a few books and magazines that I recommend for your

daily half hour of required SAT preparation reading.

Title	Why it would be helpful
Pride and Prejudice	Familiarize yourself with an older style of English. This will help with both the literature excerpts and the history excerpts on the SAT.
Stanford Alumni Magazine	Great science magazine that I used to prepare for the SAT. It publishes the issues for free online which you can access at https://alumni.stanford.edu/get/page/magazine/
The Wealth of Nations	This book will help to familiarize you with an older style of English and will prepare you well for any passages on history or economics
Unbroken	If you are someone who has not yet developed a habit of reading, this is a perfect book with which to start. It is easier to read and absolutely gripping. This book would help with history and literature passages

It is also imperative that you read your assigned reading

in school. I know that many students are in the habit of using

Sparknotes. However, you should not use Sparknotes because actually reading your assigned books will improve your SAT score. Think of doing your assigned school reading as killing two birds with one stone. You are going to improve your grade in English and your SAT score simultaneously. That's hard to beat.

Chapter 12

Preparing Like an Athlete

As a three-season varsity athlete and captain at my high school, I have learned the importance of training intelligently. Running a marathon without any preparation would be foolish. Similarly taking a test as long and strenuous as the SAT requires ample preparation. Just as with a sport, daily practice is essential for improvement. You must train your mind for the SAT just as an athlete would train his or her body.

It's essential that you live like an athlete in the weeks prior to the SAT, especially the week before the SAT. If you want to do well on the SAT, the following tips are non-negotiable:

- Turn off all technology and get it out of sight while studying for the SAT.

- Sleep for at least 7 hours every night with no technology in your room (try to get 9-10 hours every night during the week prior to the test).

- Eat healthily to allow your brain to work properly.

- Exercise regularly

- Do not procrastinate on homework because you will need time for SAT preparation. To make time for SAT prep you will likely need to cut out social media time.

SAT schedule if you have <u>four weeks</u> until the test:

	Practice testing	Reviewing Answers	Independent Reading	Total Time:
Mon	Take reading section of SAT: **65 minutes**	Check answers when finished and go over ones you got wrong: **15 minutes**	Independent reading: **30 minutes**	Total time: **1:50**
Tue	Take writing section of SAT: **35 minutes**	Same: **15 minutes**	Independent reading: **30 minutes**	Total time: **1:20**
Wed	Take math non calc section of SAT: **25 minutes**	Same: **15 minutes**	Independent reading: **30 minutes**	Total time: **1:10**
Thu	Take math calc section of SAT: **55 minutes**	Same: **15 minutes**	Independent reading: **30 minutes**	Total time: **1:40**
Fri	Take essay of SAT: **50 minutes**	Same: **15 minutes**	Independent reading: **30 minutes**	Total time: **1:35**
Sat	Take full SAT in 1 sitting: **3 hours**	Same: **15 minutes**	Independent reading: **30 minutes**	Total time: **3:45**
Sun	Day off	Day off	Independent reading: **30 minutes**	Total time: **0:30**

Repeat this for 4 weeks until the day of the SAT. This may seem like a lot of work, but just focusing and grinding it out for these for 4 weeks will be well worth it. Do not do any SAT prep the day before the SAT. Get at least 9 hours of sleep every night the week before the SAT.

SAT schedule if you have <u>several months</u> until the test

	Practice testing	Reviewing Answers	Independent Reading	Total Time:
Mon	Do 1 reading passage and the questions with it: **12 minutes**	Check answers when finished and go over ones you got wrong: **5 minutes**	Independent reading: **30 minutes**	Total time: **0:47**
Tue	Do one writing passage and the questions with it: **10 minutes**	Same: **5 minutes**	Independent reading: **30 minutes**	Total time: **0:45**
Wed	Do five math calc problems: **5 minutes**	Same: **5 minutes**	Independent reading: **30 minutes**	Total time: **0:40**
Thu	Do five math noncalc problems: **5 minutes**	Same: **5 minutes**	Independent reading: **30 minutes**	Total time: **0:40**
Fri	Day off	Day off	Independent reading: **30 minutes**	Total time: **0:30**
Sat	Take full SAT in 1 sitting: **3 hours**	Same: **30 minutes**	Independent reading: **30 minutes**	Total time: **4:00**
Sun	Day off	Day off	Independent reading: **30 minutes**	Total time: **0:30**

Repeat this for the dozen or so weeks until the day of the SAT. For practice problems during the week, buy a workbook with SAT problems or practice tests not produced by the College Board. For the complete SAT that you will take every Saturday, only use college board released tests. This lighter workload will prepare you adequately for the SAT. Do not do any SAT prep the day before the SAT. Get at least 9 hours of sleep every night the week before the SAT.

If you follow all these tips and one of these schedules, I know that you will do well on the SAT. I hope that you found this book helpful. If you did, could you do me a favor and write a review on Amazon so that others can discover this book? I would love the feedback! Also, check out my latest book, *The Authentic College Admissions Almanac,* which details how get into a top 20 university while still having a life. Feel free to email me with any questions at nathan.halberstadt@gmail.com. I love to hear from my readers! If you want to hear more from me, you can follow me on Instagram at <u>n8halberstadt</u>. Thanks!

Good luck on the exam. Onward!